The Try Not To Laugh Super Kids Challenge Joke Book

Jeff Fahnoe

The Try Not To Laugh Rules

1. Split into two teams.
2. The first team picks a random joke from book.
3. The first team reads the joke to second team.
4. The first team can use funny faces, weird voices and nutty gestures!
5. If they second team laughs, the first team gets a point.
6. Next round, the roles are reversed and the second team reads a random joke to the first team.
7. The first team that gets to five points wins!
8. Use the score sheets on the next few pages!

Game	Team 1	Team 2
1		
2		
3		
4		
5		
6		
7		
8		
9		
10		

Game	Team 1	Team 2
11		
12		
13		
14		
15		
16		
17		
18		
19		
20		

Game	Team 1	Team 2
21		
22		
23		
24		
25		
26		
27		
28		
29		
30		

Why did the bee go see the doctor?

It had hives.

What did the remote do when the TV asked her out on a date?

She turned him down!

What is green and sings?

Elvis Parsley!

Did you hear about the guy who dreamt he was a muffler?

He woke up exhausted.

What did the turkey say to the computer?

"Google, Google, Google."

Where do belly buttons go to school?
The Navel Academy!

What do you call a painting by a cat?
A paw-trait.

What do you call an elf who sings?
A wrapper!

What do spiders eat with fried chicken?
Corn on the cobweb.

What does a dragon eat with his soup?
Firecrackers!

Knock Knock.
Who's there?
Andrew.
Andrew who?
Andrew all over the walls!

What did the archer get when he hit a bullseye?
A very angry bull!

How does Steve chop down a tree with his bare hands?
How wood I know?

Why did the seagull fly north?
Because it was too far to walk.

Where do ghosts like to go swimming?
Lake Eerie.

What's the difference between a pizza and my pizza jokes?
My pizza jokes can't be topped!

How do you know you're close to a Frito Lay factory?
Because of the chips and dip in the road!

What did the celery say to the veggie dip?
I'm stalking you!

Why do seals swim in salt water?
Because pepper water makes them sneeze!

What do you call a book full of made-up words?
A "fiction-ary."

Why was the jack-o-lantern afraid to cross the road?
It had no guts!

Why is a dog's nose in the middle of its face?
Because it's the scenter!

Did you hear about the Minecraft movie?
It's going to be a Blockbuster!

What do zombies eat for dessert?
Chocolate covered aunts.

Why did the cannon have trouble finding work?

Because it kept getting fired!

Why was the fly dancing on the top of the Pepsi bottle?

Because it said, "Twist to open."

Did you know the roundest knight at King Arthur's round table was Sir Cumference?

Yep, he acquired his size from too much pi!

Why did the chicken cross the road?

To get some eggs-ercise!

**Knock Knock.
Who's there?
Queen!
Queen who?**
Queen as a whistle.

**What do you call leprechauns
who collect aluminum cans,
used newspapers and plastic
bottles?**
"Wee-cyclers!"

**Why doesn't anybody like
Dracula?**
He has a bat temper.

**What kind of fruit do calendars
love?**
Dates!

What is the best day to go to the beach?
Sunday, of course!

What do you call a traveling flea?
An itch-hiker.

How do you make an apple puff?
Chase it round the garden.

What has 3 feet but no toes?
A yardstick.

Why did the pig buy a Powerball ticket?
He wanted to be filthy rich.

Knock Knock.
Who's there?
Ice cream soda.
Ice cream soda, who?
Ice cream soda people can hear me!

What's red, white and blue?
A sad candy cane!

Where do cowboys go to think?
The ponder-osa.

What dance do women do when summer is over?
Tango (tan-go).

Where do fortunetellers dance?
At the crystal ball!

What do cats like to eat on sunny days?
Mice cream cones!

What is a toad's favorite place to eat?
Ihop!

What happens when frogs park illegally?
They get toad!

What's a cow's favorite moosical note?
Beef-flat!

What did Obi-Wan say at the rodeo?
"Use the horse, Luke!"

Why don't mummies go on vacation?
They're afraid they might unwind.

Why do news reporters hang out at the ice-cream shop?
Because they are always looking for a scoop!

Whom do monsters buy their cookies from?
The Ghoul Scouts.

Why was the scalene triangle sad?
He would never be right.

What do you call an owl with a deep voice?
A growl!

Knock Knock.
Who's there?
Ringo!
Ringo who?
Ringo round the rosie!

What is a chick's favorite drink?
Peepsi!

Why was the cell phone wearing glasses?
Because it lost its contacts.

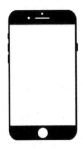

What did the ghost teacher say to her class?
"Watch the board, and I'll go through it again."

Knock Knock.
Who's there?
Oakham
Oakham who?
Oakham all ye faithful.

What did the tectonic plate say after the earthquake?
"It wasn't my fault!"

Why wasn't Noah a good card player?
Because he only had two of a kind!

What do you get when you cross a snowman and a vampire?
Frostbite!

Why do NHL players never sweat?
They have too many fans!

Why don't sharks eat clowns?
They taste funny

Why did the rock star put his guitar in the fridge?
Because he wanted to play cool music.

Do zombies eat popcorn with their fingers?
No, they eat the fingers separately.

Which are the best animals at baseball?
Score-pions.

Why did the baker go to jail?
He was caught beating an egg.

What did the stop sign say to the yield sign?
I don't know either. They were speaking in sign language.

How do you measure a joke's speed?
Smiles per hour!

What do you get if you drop a piano on an army base?
A flat major.

How do you find where a flea has bitten you?
Start from scratch!

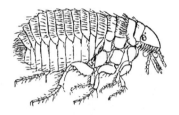

What is a flea's favorite book?
The itch-hikers guide to the galaxy!

What kind of vegetables are sold at the zoo?
Zoo-chini!

What would happen if you cut off your left side?
You would be all right.

What is the Easter Bunny's favorite state capital?
Al-bunny, New York!

What did the pig say while she was tanning?
"I'm bacon!"

Did you hear about the tanning Olympics?
Everybody tried to get bronze!

Why did the astronaut get fired?
He kept staring off into space.

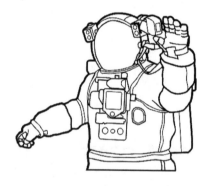

Knock Knock.
Who's there?
Yourself!
Yourself who?
Your cell phone is ringing so you better answer it!

Did you hear about the two bats on a date?

It was love at first bite!

Why did the cow jump over the moon?

Because the farmer had cold hands!

How do you throw a party for an astronaut?

You have to plan-et

Why is it hard to keep a secret down on the farm?

Because the potatoes have eyes, the corn has ears, and the beanstalk.

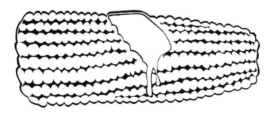

Why are frogs so good at basketball?
Because they always make jump shots!

Where do sheep go on vacation?
To the baaaaaahamas.

Why are bad school grades like a shipwreck in the Arctic Ocean?
They're both below C level!

What do you call a snowman with a six-pack?
An ab-dominal snowman.

What is a tree's least favorite month?
Sep-timber!

What happens when the fog lifts in Los Angeles, California?
UCLA!

What did Snow White say when her pictures weren't ready?
"Someday, my prints will come!"

What do you call a holiday that rabbits go on when they get married?
A Bunnymoon!

Why did Dracula take cough medicine?
To stop his coffin.

What would you get if you crossed the Easter Bunny with a famous French general?
Napoleon Bunnyparte!

Why did the deer need braces?
He had buck teeth.

Why wasn't the moon hungry?
Because it was full!

Where automobiles go for a dip?
The carpool.

Knock Knock.
Who's there?
Amish.
Amish, who?
That's funny; you don't look like a shoe!

Why did the pelican get special treatment at the restaurant?
He had a big bill.

Who did Frankenstein take to the prom?
His ghoul friend.

What kind of car does a sheep like to drive?
A Lamb-orghini.

What do you call a cow that doesn't give milk?
A milk dud.

Did you do your homework?
No, I'm saving it for a brainy day.

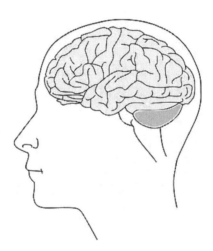

What do you call a bear with no teeth?
A gummy bear!

What do you call a cow with no legs at all?
Ground beef!

What did the pirate say to the sumo wrestler?
You sure arrrrr big!

Did you hear about the fight in the kitchen?
A fish got battered!

Why did the chicken cross the ocean?
To get to the other tide!

What did the reindeer say to the football player?

"Your Blitzen days are over!"

Knock Knock.
Who's There?
Debbie!
Debbie Who?

Debbie or not to be, that is the question!

How do you protect a jewelry store at night?

You locket.

What happened when the skunk wrote a book?

It became a best smeller!

What did the leopard say after a big meal?
"That sure hits the spots!"

How did it feel when the racer crashed through the window?
Very pane-ful!

Why did the policeman give the sheep a ticket?
He was a baaaaaaaad driver.

What did the big chimney say to the little chimney?
"You're too young to smoke!"

Knock Knock.
Who's there?
Little old lady
Little Old lady who?
I didn't know you cold yodel!

Did you hear about the
hamburger that couldn't stop
making jokes?
He was on a roll!

Why was the broom late?
It over-swept.

Why did the cupcake go to the doctor?
It had frost-bite!

What do you call a powerful prehistoric explosive?
Dino-mite!

What smells the best at a Thanksgiving dinner?
Your nose.

Why did the teacher stop the shoelace?
It was being knotty.

Why don't ducks tell jokes while they're flying?

Because they quack up.

What do you get when you cross a fishing lure with a gym sock?

A hook, line and stinker!

How does a restaurant get the freshest ingredients?

They cut a dill.

How do astronauts eat their ice creams?

In floats!

What has 18 legs and catches flies?
A baseball team!

Why did the two knives go to the dance together?
Because they both looked sharp!

Why does Peter Pan always fly?
Because he Neverlands!

How do you get the salad party started?
With a phat beet.

Who do you call when a rabbit needs a haircut?

The hare dresser.

What's a kidney's favorite instrument?

An organ.

What is a boxer's favorite part of the joke?

The "punch" line!

What do you get when a cow jumps over the fence?

Udder destruction.

What is a bear's favorite drink?
Koka-Koala!

What do cats wear at night?
Paw-jamas!

What do cannibals eat at parties?
Buttered host.

Why can't you play cards in the jungle?
Because there are too many cheetahs.

How do people swimming in the ocean say "hi" to each other?

They wave!

Which colonists told the most jokes?

Punsylvanians!

What do you call a short fortuneteller on the run?

A small medium at large.

If the Pilgrims came on the Mayflower then what did the teachers come on?

The scholar ships.

Knock Knock.
Who's there?
Monkey.
Monkey, who?
Monkey won't fit, that's why I knocked.

What did one red blood cell say to another?
"All this work is in vein!"

What do lawyers wear to formal dinners?
Lawsuits!

How do monsters tell their future?
They read their horror-scope.

What tree has the flu all the time?
A sycamore.

What do you call a blueberry that uses foul language?
Berry rude!

How do you fix a broken tuba?
With a tuba glue.

What did one elevator say to the other?
"I think I'm coming down with something!"

What did the balloon say to the doctor?
"I feel lightheaded!"

When is an Irish Potato not an Irish Potato?
When it's a French fry!

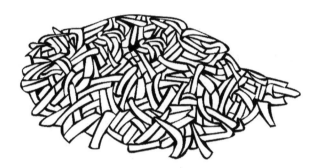

What do call a cow that has just had a calf?
Decalfenated

What street do lions live on?
Mane Street.

What do you call a fly with no wings?
A walk.

Why did the orange go to the doctor?
It wasn't peeling well!

What do you call a fake noodle?
An impasta!

What goes snap, crackle, and pop?
A firefly with a short circuit.

Knock Knock.
Who's there?
Alex!
Alex who?
Alex the questions round here!

What do you call a duck that steals?
A robber ducky.

Why did the mushroom get invited to all the parties?
Because he was a fungi!

What is a cat's favorite musical instrument?
Purr-cussion.

What's the quietest sport in the world?

Bowling, because you can always hear a pin drop!

What do you call two spiders that just got married?

Newlywebs!

What is the difference between a piano and a fish?

You can tune a piano but you cannot tuna fish.

Why do demons and ghouls hang out together?

Because demons are a ghoul's best friend!

What does a vampire never order at a restaurant?

A stake sandwich.

Why didn't the skeleton dance at the disco?

He had no body to dance with!

Where is the only place Friday comes before Thursday?

The dictionary!

What do you call an egg from outer space?
An "egg-stra terrestrial".

What do you call a bee that's had a spell put on him?
Bee-witched!

Where do ghosts play tennis?
On a tennis corpse!

What do you call a belt with a watch on it?
A waist of time

How do you make a fish laugh?
Tell a whale of a tale!

How many birds does it take to change a light bulb?
Toucan do it.

What's a cat's favorite button on the TV remote?
Paws.

What do you get when you run in front of a car?
Tired.

What did the boat dock say when it was arrested?
"I demand a jury of my piers."

DOCTOR: How did you get here so fast?
PATIENT: Flu.

What makes a mouth sad?
A tongue depressor.

How can you find a dogwood tree?
By its bark.

What do you call a sushi roll that sings pop music?
Spicy autotuna.

What did the bee say to the naughty bee?
Bee-hive yourself!

What has four wheels and flies?
A garbage truck.

Why did the farmer have to separate the chicken and the turkey?
He sensed fowl play.

What do you call a bee who is having a bad hair day?
A Frizz-bee.

How did the strawberries start their band?
They just got together and jammed.

What is a balloon's least favorite school activity?
A pop quiz.

What's a truck full of bison?
A buffa-load!

What do you call Chewbacca when he has chocolate stuck in his hair?
A Chocolate Chip Wookiee.

Why didn't anyone laugh at the gardener's jokes?
Because they were too corny!

How did the grizzly catch the fish?
With his bear hands.

Did you hear about the kidnapping?
He woke up.

How do bees get to school?
On the school buzz!

Why does everyone need bread and water?
Loaf makes the world go round.

What is a dinosaur's least favorite reindeer?
Comet.

Which state are pencils from?
Pencil-vania!

I really love hotels.
If you love them so much, why don't you Marriott?

What's a monster's favorite dessert?
I scream!

What do you call the skeleton in the closet?
Last year's hide-and-seek winner!

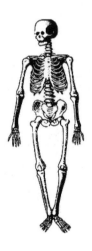

What nursery rhyme do they sing in the Himalayas?
Yak and Jill.

What do you give a sick horse?
Cough stirrup!

What do you call a dog on the farm?
A corn dog.

How much money does a skunk have?
One scent!

What do you call a fish with no eyes?
"A fsh."

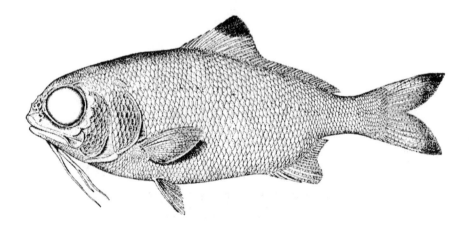

How do you know when a clock is hungry?

When it goes back for seconds.

Why did the cops go to the softball game?

Because they heard someone was stealing a base.

THE END!

34325786R00035

Made in the USA
Lexington, KY
21 March 2019